The River Girl

Wendy Cope

Illustrated by Nicholas Garland

ff

faber and faber
LONDON · BOSTON

First published in Great Britain in 1991
by Faber and Faber Limited
3 Queen Square London WC1N 3AU

Photoset by Wilmaset, Birkenhead, Wirral
Printed in Great Britain by
Clays Ltd, St Ives plc

Wendy Cope is hereby identified as the author of this work
and Nicholas Garland as the illustrator of this work
in accordance with Section 77 of the Copyright,
Design and Patents Act 1988.

A CIP record for this book is available from the British Library.

ISBN: 0–571–16062–X
0–571–16136–7 (Pbk)

The River Girl

about the author

Wendy Cope was educated at Farringtons School and at
Oxford, where she read history. She worked as a primary
school teacher for a number of years, and encouraging
children to write rekindled her own interest in poetry. Her
first collection of poems, *Making Cocoa for Kingsley Amis*
(Faber and Faber, 1986), was a bestseller. In 1987 she won
a Cholmondeley Award for poetry. Since then she has
published a collection of finger rhymes for children,
Twiddling Your Thumbs (Faber and Faber, 1988).

about the illustrator

Nicholas Garland studied fine art at the Slade School. His
career began in the theatre, where he worked as a stage
manager and, later, as a director. It was in 1966 that he
joined the *Daily Telegraph* as their political cartoonist. He
moved to the *Independent* in 1986, then back to the
Telegraph in 1991. He is the author of *Not Many Dead:
Journal of a Year in Fleet Street* (Hutchinson, 1990), as well
as having several illustrated books to his credit, including a
collection of his political drawings — *Cartoons* (Salamander
Press, 1984).

by the same author

MAKING COCOA FOR KINGSLEY AMIS
TWIDDLING YOUR THUMBS
(for young children)

edited by Wendy Cope

IS THAT THE NEW MOON?
(An anthology of women's poetry
for teenagers)

The River Girl is based on a plot outline by Gren Middleton of the Movingstage Marionette Company, who commissioned the poem for performance. The author wishes to thank Gren, and Juliet Middleton, his partner in the company, for the idea, and for their kindness and encouragement.

The River Girl

An English meadow, early in the morning.
The Thames has whispered through another night
And now the sun is coming out and touching
The water and the grass with summer light.

The river rises in a shallow valley
And flows across our green and pleasant land
Two hundred miles and more until fresh water
Turns salt, and muddy banks give way to sand.

In Gloucestershire a stream, it meets the ocean
A mighty thoroughfare, deep, wide and strong.
It knew our forbears. It will know our children.
Sweet Thames run softly till I end my song.

And who is this, who sits beside the river
Day after day and gazes at the sky
With searching eyes and gazes at the water
And frowns and shakes his head with many a sigh?

A would-be poet, seeking inspiration.
He has a notebook. Every page is white
And blank. He sits and sits and dreams of greatness.
He dreams of greatness but he cannot write.

And yet the merest glance tells the observer
That here's a man devoted to his art —
Long hair, pale face and crumpled corduroy trousers.
He knows a thing or two. He looks the part.

Beneath the river's smooth and quiet surface,
Where fishes play and water-weeds unfurl
In dappled sunlight, lives the lovely Isis,
Giver of dreams, enchantress, river girl.

As soon as Isis sees the handsome poet,
She breaks the surface. Floating in a dress
Of purest white, she's graceful as a lily
(Where most of us, of course, would look a mess).

The handsome poet sees the lovely Isis
And gasps and cannot take his eyes away.
He smiles. She smiles. It is an old, old story.
Love at first sight. It happens every day.

Oh, love's a powerful, fast-moving current
That seizes us before we've time to think.
And some of us it carries on to safety
Upon a happy shore, while others sink.

And these two? We shall see. She floats towards him
As, silently, he stretches out his hand.
She takes it and he tries to pull her to him.
She shakes her head. He doesn't understand.

'Oh come and walk with me, enchanting maiden.
Climb up this bank. Enjoy the summer weather.
Like young lambs, we will frolic in the meadows.
Oh come, let us be lyrical together.

'Your hair will dry and gleam like finest satin.
I'll gather flowers and make a little crown
And place it on your head and call you "Princess" –
Good heavens. Hang on. I must write this down.'

He lets her go and scribbles in his notebook.
A miracle! He is in love and *writing*.
When he looks up and smiles, his eyes are blazing –
'My love. My Muse. Oh, this is so exciting.'

She smiles as well. And, since she has a secret,
She looks a little bit like La Gioconda,
Which does no harm at all. His heart turns over,
With every passing second he grows fonder.

'My love is like a young and tender sapling.
My love is like a rose without a thorn.
Coming to banish misery and darkness,
My love is like the first light of the dawn.

'These words! Where are they coming from, my darling?'
She knows, says nothing, looks down at the river.
For if he guesses, or if she should tell him,
So much the worse for her. Fear makes her shiver.

'You're cold, my love. Please come and sit beside me.
I want to keep you warm and safe and never
Let go of you. You're beautiful. You're magic.
Come here, come now, and stay with me for ever.

'Your eyes are saying yes, though you are silent.'
He grasps her hand again. He grasps her shoulder
And kisses her, and kissing gives such pleasure,
He cannot help but grow a little bolder.

She breaks away. 'My love, I have to go now.
Be here tomorrow and we'll meet again.
The night will seem too long. I'll count the minutes
And think about you all the time till then.'

'Don't go. Don't go. I beg you, do not leave me
Alone, to suffer passionate distress.
Look, are you on the phone? Give me your number.'
'There's no phone where I'm going.' 'Your address?'

But as he speaks, she's vanished underwater
And, surfacing a hundred yards downstream,
She calls to him. 'My darling. Do not follow.
We'll meet tomorrow. Now go home and dream.'

'Go home and dream.' He turns away and murmurs
Like one bewitched, and walks towards the town.
'Go home and dream.' He is already dreaming
Of kisses and . . . No. Best not write it down.

This is for families. Let's say he's happy.
He is in love, he's lost, on fire, possessed.
We'll leave him wandering dreamily to Oxford,
His notebook clasped to his impassioned breast.

We'll leave the world we know and follow Isis
Into her world, the kingdom underwater
That's ruled by Father Thames. And she must find him –
Our heroine is Father Thames's daughter,

Adopted by him when she was a baby
But that was many centuries ago.
You wonder who she is and where she came from
And why? Ask Father Thames. I do not know.

But I can tell you that he loves her dearly –
Though he can be forbidding, angry, cold,
He loves his daughter. She's his joy, his treasure.
He'd like to keep her with him, now he's old.

But he is wise, too wise to think a daughter
Can be contented with a father's love.
He dreads the day some other love will beckon
And call his Isis to the world above.

'Where are you, Father?' He can hear her calling –
A distant cry at first, then it comes near.
'O Father! Father!' – breathless and excited –
He stands up tall. He will not show his fear.

He stands up tall and welcomes her. 'My daughter!'
She looks at him and sees his face is stern.
She hesitates. Will he be understanding
Or spoil it all with fatherly concern?

Oh why is he so strict and so old-fashioned?
She is afraid to speak, now she has found him.
She'd better kneel and take his hand and kiss it –
Such gestures often help her get around him.

And when she's kissed his hand, she gazes at him
Most solemnly. She's wide-eyed with respect.
And when his aged face begins to soften,
She knows all this is having some effect.

'Arise, my daughter. We will sit together –
I am an old man and I need to rest.
And you can tell me why you're so excited,
Although I think I have already guessed.'

'Father, I met a man.' He nods. 'Continue.'
'He is the one for me. I'm sure, I know it.
If you could see his face! He's good. He's noble
And handsome. Father, this man is a poet!'

Her father sighs. It's worse than he expected.
To lose her to a man at all is bad
But to a poet! He has seen these poets
In action. 'Father, you look very sad.

'Dear Father, I have never disobeyed you.
I love you and remember what you said –
That I must never, never leave the river –
And when he asked me to, I shook my head.

'But now I have to ask you for my freedom
To come and go.' She's trying not to cry.
'I promise that I'll come and see you often
But if I'm not with him, I think I'll die.'

'My child, my child, now calm yourself and listen.
I am too old to think that anyone
Can argue with a young girl's love. A parent
May just as well attempt to quench the sun.

'If you have lost your heart, I can't retrieve it,
So I will let you go, yes, with my blessing.
But first I have a gift for you, to help you
To fascinate this poet and keep him guessing.

'The magic powers you possess already
Enable you, dear child, to be a giver
Of words and dreams. Today I will enhance them
Before you leave me and our lovely river.'

He stands. 'Now, Isis, come and stand before me.'
He grasps her head and holds it very tight,
Closes his eyes, and, fierce with concentration,
He speaks so loudly that the fish take fright.

'You powers that rule the rivers and the oceans,
You powers from whom my magic power stems,
Now manifest yourselves in these quiet waters.
I summon you to help me, Father Thames.'

And suddenly the water all around them
Grows turbulent. 'Spirits, now you are here
I ask you to confer the gift of changing
Upon this river girl, my child so dear.

'Give her the power to transform her body
Into the shape of any living thing –
Of furry beast, or bird or fish or flower,
So she may hide, be fierce, run fast, take wing.'

He moves away from Isis, leaves her standing
Alone. The turbulence intensifies.
It closes round her and becomes a vortex.
'I want . . . I want to be a fish!' she cries.

No sooner said than done. Now she is breathing
Through gills. She flaps her fins and tail with grace.
The water's calm again. She swims to Father
And plants a fishy kiss upon his face,

Then swims away and hides behind a boulder
And, when she reappears, she is herself.
She laughs, delighted with her own performance.
Her father smiles. She's still his little elf.

But when he speaks, he's serious and solemn.
'If this man marries you, he will grow strong.
Now go and find him. Go and find your poet.
Come back and visit me before too long.'

He holds her to his breast, then turns abruptly
And strides away, upright, his head held high.
And Isis suddenly feels very lonely
And sad. 'Goodbye, Old Father Thames, goodbye.'

At last she turns away and swims down-river,
Leaving her happy childhood world behind
And looking forward to a happy future.
Good luck, sweet maiden, and may life be kind.

Six months have passed. Our lovers now are married,
Living together in a little flat.
He writes and writes. She is his Muse and soulmate.
The cooking and the housework? She does that.

And she is happy just to be beside him
And when her lovely eyes meet his, they shine.
And every time he looks upon his darling,
He dreams up yet another telling line.

It's wonderful. His writer's block has melted –
Since he met her, he's had so much to say
That he has filled up notebook after notebook
And words are dancing in his head all day.

And words are singing of the world around him –
How beautiful it is, for now he sees
With lover's eyes, and everything is altered.
He's come alive. He's growing like the trees.

He's opening like flowers in the sunshine,
He's flowing like the river, sure and strong,
And, what is more, some people think it likely
That he will be in print before too long.

Last month he sent his work to Tite and Snobbo,
The publishers. Now he must wait and wonder
If it will go down well with that famed poet,
Tite's editor, the dreaded Clinton Thunder.

He knows it's good but will Clint Thunder like it?
Or will he have to try the Hatchet Press
Up North, or even Doolittle and Dalley?
And what if nobody at all says yes?

'A cup of tea, my love?' 'Oh, Isis, thank you.
Just what I wanted. Has the postman been?'
'Not yet. He's late.' 'He's late and you are lovely.
I want to kiss you, darling wife, my queen.'

Yes, they are happy. Long may they remain so.
He hears a noise and looks up. 'What was that?'
'The post?' 'Now keep your fingers crossed, my angel.'
He runs to see what's landed on the mat.

'It's here! It's here! This is from Tite and Snobbo!'
Opening it, he shakes with hope and fear.
'Yes, it's from Thunder. And he likes my poems
And says they want to publish me next year!

'Yoo hoo! Yoo hoo!' He's jumping on the armchairs,
He's dancing round the room. 'Come and be kissed,
My Muse, my love, my life, my inspiration,
Your husband's on the Tite and Snobbo list!'

Isis is overwhelmed. He finds a hanky
And wipes the tears from her beloved face,
And strokes her hair and puts his arms around her
And holds her in a long, long, long embrace.

25

The planet Earth has made another journey
Around the sun, the seasons came and went,
Things grew and died. In due course Tite and Snobbo
Produced the book. A publishing event!

The critics loved it and the public bought it
And it won three awards. Of course, such glory
Is very rarely won by any poet –
Remember that this is a fairy story.

And there is something that the storyteller
Forgot to mention. It's the hero's name:
He's called John Didde. That's D–I–D–D–E, yes,
A little like John Donne, of greater fame.

But now John Didde, too, is a name to conjure
At dinner, if you're up to date and arty.
And he is in demand. Young John and Isis
Spend every other evening at some party,

Where he is lionized by men and women:
'John Didde! Congratulations! Lovely book!'
'John Didde! I have been desperate to meet you.
I, too, write poems. Would you take a look?'

'Excuse me. I must have a word with John here.
Some time soon, could I do an interview?'
'Of course. Now here's my wife. I'll introduce you.'
She looks at Isis coldly. 'How do you do?'

Poor Isis wanders off into a corner.
She's trying not to sulk but she'd prefer
To be at home, away from all these people,
Though, even there, things aren't quite what they were.

He's made a lot of new friends, mostly poets,
Who visit him and talk for hours on end
About who's good, who's second-rate, who's dreadful.
I feel for her. It drives me round the bend

And I'm supposed to *be* a poet. Sometimes
They're rude enough to make poor Isis weep.
Her husband drinks an awful lot of whisky
And, when the last one leaves, he falls asleep.

He's lively now. He's talking to that woman.
Look at her face, at those seductive eyes.
'No, jealousy is ugly. I'm above it.
I'm Isis of the River Thames.' She sighs.

'I'm Isis of the River Thames. O Father,
In all this time I've only seen you twice.
There was so much to do. Time passed so quickly.
You might have given me some good advice.

'I've left it far too long. I'll come tomorrow
To your cool, quiet river-world and tell
My sorrows, with my head upon your shoulder,
And ask you what to do, and listen well.'

Down, down into the half-light of the river,
Isis dives. The water strokes her limbs
And she remembers how she loves to be here.
She turns a somersault and swims and swims,

As lithe as any fish. And all the creatures
Who see her pass are happy that she's here.
The bolder fishes nuzzle her in friendship
And one forgets himself and bites her ear.

'Ouch! Stop it! I am looking for my father.
Do you know where he is?' They swim ahead,
Her pilots, to the underwater bower
Where he lies sleeping on the riverbed.

He's sleeping soundly, and he looks so peaceful
She doesn't like to wake him. She prefers
To sit beside him and enjoy the water
And listen to its music, till he stirs.

'Isis, my darling girl. Am I still dreaming?
Give me your hand. I think it's really you.
At last you've come to see your poor old father
And brought that smile of yours. Ah yes. It's true.

'And how's your poet? Loving, kind and faithful?
Treating his lovely wife the way he should?
Behaving better than the other poets?'
'The truth is, Father, things are not too good.

'He's doing well. He has become quite famous
And lots of people want to know him now.
He's not the same. I feel as if I've lost him.
I want to win him back. I don't know how.'

'Oh this is sad but it does not surprise me.'
His arm's around her. They sit side by side.
'Pity the woman with a human husband.
Pity most of all the poet's bride.'

'He's very insecure.' 'I do not doubt it.'
'I think that if he lost me, he'd be sad,
But nowadays he flirts with other women
And drinks too much.' 'Isis, all poets are mad.

'Do you still love him?' 'Yes, I love him, Father.'
'Then listen carefully to my advice.
This poet owes a lot to you and sometimes
Those who give too freely pay a price.

'There is wisdom in the human saying:
"It's easier to give than to receive."
He knows you are his Muse and inspiration
And wonders what will happen, if you leave.

'And no man wants to feel he is dependent
Upon his wife. Sometimes, perhaps, he thinks
It's all too easy. He can't understand it.
He turns his back on you. He flirts. He drinks.

'From now on, Isis, be a little sparing
And cunning in the way you use your powers.
Clever Muses sometimes leave their poets
Suffering despair for hours and hours

'Or days or weeks or months.' 'Oh, that is cruel!'
'It is. Perhaps a day or two's enough.
My daughter, you are generous and loving.
Your father should have taught you to be tough.

'Do not forget the wedding-gift I gave you.
It may be useful in your hour of need.
But never let him know you have the power
To change yourself. He must not know. Take heed.'

'Father, I knew you'd help. I kneel and thank you.
Things will be better now. I'm sure.' 'We'll see.
Go live a little longer with your husband
And, if it doesn't work, come back to me.'

John Didde at home with literary cronies,
All well away on whisky, wine and beer.
And where is Isis? She is in the kitchen.
No one will notice that she isn't here.

'You're telling me, John – are you? – quite sincerely,
You think Clint Thunder's *good*? I disagree,'
Says one, in drunken tones. 'I hate the bastard.
If he knew anything, he'd publish *me*.

'Ha. Ha.' He laughs a drunken laugh and staggers
Out to another room. He's feeling ill.
'What are you working on, John?' asks a woman.
'Not much. Not much. Some days the output's nil.'

'But everybody says you're so prolific.'
'I was. But now, it seems, I'm slowing down.'
'Too many lunches?' Look, her eyes are twinkling.
'Perhaps. Too many journeys up to town.'

They smile at one another very fondly.
The others watch. Is something going on?
Suddenly a cat runs from the kitchen,
Miaowing. Jumping up, it lands on John.

'This wretched cat. I don't know where it comes from.'
He picks it up and puts it on the floor.
It leaps again and curls up on the woman.
'Ah, Moggy. What a nice puss. Shake a paw.'

The cat snarls nastily. Its claws look vicious.
Is it going to scratch the lady's face?
The lady squeals and John comes to the rescue.
'Cat. Out of here. Get out. You're in disgrace.'

They get back to their literary chatter.
The kitchen door is opening, just a crack,
While through the other door a body slouches –
A very drunken poet, coming back.

Slowly, slowly making for the sofa.
Another step or two and he'll be there.
A dark shape streaks across the room and trips him.
He's on the sofa, bottom in the air.

Oh what a sound! What fearsome, dreadful groaning!
The others pick him up and sit him down.
'Who tripped me, John?' 'It was that cat, the beggar.'
'The cat,' he echoes, with a drunken frown.

'That cat,' says John. 'It looks as if it's laughing.
Look at it. It's not sorry. No, it's glad!'
'Is it a he or she?' inquires another,
'And what's its name?' 'Don't know. I call it BAD!'

Poor cat. She slinks away into the kitchen.
Am I quite sure the cat's a she? Oh, yes.
She's got it wrong. She wanted some attention
And went too far with all this naughtiness.

'Time to be off.' 'Me too. I must be going.'
'Where's Isis, John? We ought to say goodbye.'
'It doesn't matter. I expect she's sleeping.'
'She doesn't want to talk to us.' 'She's shy.'

'Well, thanks a lot. It was a lovely evening.'
John goes along and sees them down the stairs,
And Isis reappears, out of the kitchen.
She tidies things away and pats the chairs.

'I thought you were in bed.' 'No, in the kitchen.'
'I see. You know that wretched cat got in.
You must have seen it.' Isis doesn't answer.
She cannot lie. She gives a little grin.

'I'm turning in. I'm tired. Goodnight, darling.'
'John.' 'What?' 'It doesn't matter. Go and sleep.
I won't be long.' She sits down, crying – softly,
For no man likes to hear a woman weep,

Especially if he's the cause. But, Isis,
You must not cry all night. You need some rest.
Perhaps things will be better in the morning.
Perhaps all this will turn out for the best.

Perhaps not. But we have to manage somehow.
We tell ourselves, to keep despair away,
That things can seem much better in the morning
And that tomorrow is another day.

Tomorrow never comes. Today's beginning
And John is up. He's packed a little bag.
'Are you going somewhere?' Isis asks him.
'I need to go to London. It's a drag.'

'I'll be a day or two.' 'You didn't tell me.'
'I have to go. Now please don't make a scene.
You'll be all right and I'll be back by Friday.
I'll tell you what I've done and where I've been.'

He leaves the room. His wife, at last, is angry,
Too angry to be sensible, and that
Is why she calls once more upon the spirits:
'Change me! Change me! I want to be a cat!'

When John comes back, there is no sign of Isis,
Just this fierce, snarling animal. 'Oh no!
I've had enough. This time, cat, it's the basket.'
He fetches it and grabs her. 'In you go.'

'Miaow! Miaow!' John finds a pen and paper.
'Isis, where are you? Got to go. Please try
To find a good home for this noisy creature,
As far away as possible. Goodbye.'

He rushes out and slams the door behind him.
'Miaow! Miaow!' What can poor Isis do?
Her body's far too big for this small basket.
She can't change back. She gives a piteous mew

And then falls silent. There's no one to feed her.
She's trapped. But look. Can you see what I see?
Old Father Thames! Is this a dream? A vision?
'If it doesn't work, come back to me.

'Come back to me. Come back to me, my daughter.'
He disappears without another word
And Isis acts. This monstrous caterwauling
Means something. 'Spirits! Come! Make me a bird!'

The caterwauling stops. Now she is hopping
Around the basket. 'Tap, tap', go her feet.
Yes, Isis is a bird. She is a swallow.
Her feathers shine. And she can sing. 'T-weet.'

And now it's easy to escape. She squeezes
Her avian body through a narrow hole.
She looks around her. Everything's enormous.
She shakes herself and takes a little stroll,

Then flaps her wings a bit and soon she's flying,
Soaring, swooping, landing on the floor,
And hovering, at last, before John's photo.
She gazes. She won't see him any more.

For she is leaving. Yes, she has decided.
Sad, that this is how it has to be.
She turns and flies towards an open window
And out into the sky. She's gone. She's free.

Over gardens, over streets and rooftops,
Past dreaming spires and towers, Isis flies.
Our enchanting princess of the river
Has become a princess of the skies.

Over woods and ponds and hills and meadows
Until she comes at last to that same place
Where once there sat a young and handsome poet
With an unhappy frown upon his face.

Gracefully the swallow skims the river,
Then, landing on a bough, she rests her wings.
'T-weet. T-weet.' She's calling to the spirits.
'T-weet. I want to be myself,' she sings.

48

Isis of the River Thames is standing
Upon the river bank, her head held high,
Older and wiser than the simple maiden
Who gave her heart away. Now, say goodbye —

For Isis won't be back, not in our lifetime.
One day, perhaps, when several hundred years
Have healed the wound, she'll meet our children's children
Beside the Thames. She dives and disappears.

Now who is this who walks beside the river
Day after day, and gazes at the sky
With searching eyes and gazes at the water
And weeps and shakes his head with many a sigh?

Ah John, poor John. When he got back from London,
He looked for Isis. He looked everywhere.
Weeks, months have passed and still he goes on hoping
That one day he'll come home and find her there

And take her in his arms and say he loves her.
Tormented by self-hatred and regret,
He haunts the places where they went together
And most of all this place, where first they met.

The sky is weeping too. The water's rising.
It is as if the Thames cannot contain
Such grief. The river's high and overflowing
Until the fields are lakes of tears and rain.

When they tell the story of this summer,
You'll hear about the weather and the flood
And how the River Thames at last retreated
And how the sun came out and dried the mud

And life went on. Poor John will manage somehow
And one day, maybe, you will chance to find
A copy of his book. Within its pages,
Isis still enchants the human mind.

Now they sleep, and hidden hands are resting.
It's almost time for you to go, dear friends.
A swallow sings. The sun sets on the river.
Sweet Thames run softly as our story ends.